The Wound Dresser

Books by Jack Coulehan

The Knitted Glove (1991)

First Photographs of Heaven (1995)

The Heavenly Ladder (2000)

Medicine Stone (2002)

Bursting with Danger and Music (2012)

The Wound Dresser

Jack Coulehan

Library of Congress Cataloging-in-Publication Data
Names: Coulehan, John L., 1943-, author.
Title: The wound dresser / Jack Coulehan.
Description: Albuquerque, NM : JB Stillwater Publishing Company, [2016]
Identifiers: LCCN 2016020740 (print) | LCCN 2016025297 (ebook) | ISBN
    9781937240738 (pbk.) | ISBN 9781937240745 (epub)
Classification: LCC PS3603.O88 A6 2016 (print) | LCC PS3603.O88 (ebook) | DDC
    811/.6--dc23
LC record available at https://lccn.loc.gov/2016020740

20160601

JB Stillwater Publishing Company
12901 Bryce Ave NE
Albuquerque, NM 87112

Printed in the United States of America

This book is for Anne, my best friend and life's companion

Acknowledgements

Robert Pinsky, Poet Laureate of the United States from 1997 to 2000, selected *The Wound Dresser* as a finalist for the 2016 Dorset Poetry Prize.

I wish to thank the editors of journals in which the following poems were first published. In some cases they appeared in earlier versions or with different titles:

Annals of Internal Medicine: "The Biopsy Room: Prostate," "Doctor Barrone," "He Lectures at the Heritage Association Dinner," "Family History," "The Ghost," "A Lesson in Diagnosis," "Ockham's Razor," "The Secret of the Care," "The Testimony of Mary Clues' Daughter," "Theories of the Soul," "To the Heart of Lazar Riverius, Galenist Physician," "Two of Them," "Unsettled Weather," and "War Remnants Museum, Ho Chi Minh City." *Antietam Review:* "Ascension Thursday." *Birmingham Review*: "Poem for David." *Canadian Medical Association Journal:* "Aesculapius Writes His Memoirs" and "Eight Hands." *Dickinson Review:* "Los Locos." *The Examined Life:* "Corrigan and the Giant." *Journal of the American Medical Association (JAMA):* "Alternative Medicine," "Anita and Vladimir," "Cesium 137," "The Exterior Palace," "Fever of Unknown Origin," "Incomplete Knowledge," "Livedo Reticularis," "A Long Shot," "McGonigle's Foot," "March of Dimes Girl, 1954," "Metamorphosis," "A Narrow Escape," "On Reading Walt Whitman's 'The Wound Dresser,'" "The Queen of Sweden," "Ralph Angelo Attends the Barbeque," "The Rock," "Sacrament of the Sick," "Sts. Cosmas and Damien Perform the First Human Leg Transplant," "The Second Act," and "Take Off Your Clothes." *The Journal (Ohio State University):* "Appetite." *The Lancet,* "Christmas in Kosovo." *The Lumen:* "Physical Diagnosis." *Parting Gifts:*

"To the Mummy of a Thief in the Crypt of St. Michan's, Dublin." *The Pharos:* "Role Model." *Pulse: Voices From the Heart of Medicine:* "Retrospective." *South Coast Poetry Journal:* "Shall Inherit."

Earlier versions of "McGonigle's Foot," "The Rule of Thirds," "To the Mummy of a Thief in the Crypt of St. Michan's Church, Dublin," and "Icon of the Heavenly Ladder" appeared in the chapbook *The Heavenly Ladder* (2001).

I am especially grateful to Patti Tana for her invaluable help in preparing *The Wound Dresser* for publication.

And whoever walks a furlong without sympathy walks to his own funeral dressed in his shroud....

Walt Whitman, "Song of Myself," Section 48

Contents

TWO

THREE

FOUR

On Reading Walt Whitman's "The Wound Dresser"

You dampen dressings with warm water,
detach them from dried blood and debris,
carefully removing layers of gauze
without a gown, without gloves. An attendant
stands behind you with a bucket of soiled
bandages and shifts impatiently
from one foot to the other while you work.

You lean close to a soldier's yellow-blue
countenance, inserting his shattered language
into a letter addressed to his sweetheart.
When his whisper drops off, you suggest,
though never in haste, a word for the text.
You camp on a stool beside the cot,
observing your man, embracing the scene.

I stop at the foot of each cot and check
its numbers and charts. This body, wasted
and sinking, is next. I ask and record,
examine and plan, confident that signs
I interpret tell the truth. You remain
tinkering at your soldier's side, as I step
to the next cot and the cot after that.

ONE

The Secret of the Care

In those days I wore vestments to clinic —
pressed white pants, crisp shirt and jacket,
symbols of purity, though magnets
for stains, pockets puffed with instruments
and memory aids. I began by asking
questions, while fumbling my notes.
I squinted into the patients' lenses
for sclerotic vessels. I palpated
their abdomens, ballotted their livers,
and listened to respiratory crackles,
while disguising the depth of my doubt
with a kindly, but serious look.
It was difficult. I was surprised to find
how much I disliked some of the patients —
rude and demanding, manipulative,
violent and dense. Shrinking violets
that made me squirm. Paranoid addicts.
And a few that goaded my deep anger.
I tried to remember to step away.
The secret of the care of the patient,
professors had told me, *lies in caring
for the patient,* a maxim I was certain
cut to the core of healing. In time,
I convinced himself, all this rigmarole
of anger and hurt would work itself out.
I'd grow in wisdom. I'd ascend
to a higher, more open plane. Headache,
anger, fatigue, and doubt would disappear.
It's bound to get easier, I thought.

Incomplete Knowledge

Pretending it didn't hurt, he got up
from his recliner and held out the film
he had badgered his doctor to give him.

By the dim lamp, the x-ray disclosed
a fuzzy coalescence where his left lung
should have been. And fluid on the right.

My father-in-law asked what I thought
of the situation, while commenting
in a casual voice that he had decided

on radiation, a plan the oncologist
had convinced him would be effective.
I stared at clusters of finger smudges

on the film's surface — they irked me.
His face, drained now that its padding
had disappeared, seemed spiritual.

His cigarette hand fluttered above
his breast pocket for a pack. I nodded.
Radiation, I said, *is the best choice.*

A Lesson in Diagnosis

Inspection

We snap on both lights and shake him
until he wakes. To get a good look
we make him flip to the prone position
and untie his gown. Amazing! Well-worth
the extra trip. His lesions blanket
the upper back like thousands of fish eggs
in a salmon-colored cloud. Among them
are jagged claws of excoriations —
he can't stop scratching. Even drugs
don't calm him down. His only comfort
is sleep. Sleep and studio wrestling.

Palpation

By the time it's my turn to palpate
her spleen, the skin that stretches over its
rocky surface has angered with hard use.
The map of Ohio she hides behind
to ignore us flinches when I begin,
and before I finish, she drops a pair
of spectacles pincered in her left hand
to the floor. Myers is fuming at how long
we're taking. He drags us to another case —
this one, a supraclavicular mass.
No one stoops to pick up her glasses.

Percussion

To demonstrate percussion, Myers drums
on the patient's abdominal swelling
with her in the supine position.
He orders us to listen for the note
to change, but I'm captured by the field
of heaped-up irregular scars.
How many times has she been stabbed?
Myers repositions her and drums again.
This time the dullness has descended,
showing the fluid is free and subject
to gravity. Fluid? I imagine magma
about to erupt, her belly button
blowing its top. During the discussion
she keeps trying without success
to cover her nakedness with a sheet.

Auscultation

I stand too close to the patient's bed
to escape Myers insisting I be first
to listen to the man's heart and describe
its murmur — sharp and diamond-shaped
or continuous? I'm embarrassed
to confess that beneath my stethoscope
a dozen bats flutter from their cave
at sundown, their eerie flaps almost too soft
for me to pick up. After a pause
I say, *systolic murmur, diamond-shaped.*
Myers twitches his upper lip at the lie.

Corrigan and the Giant

What victory! Corrigan's lymphoma
has melted away with an extract
of periwinkle, like the Wicked Witch
in *The Wizard of Oz.* Corrigan's tumor
had bulged behind his breast and twisted
his trachea. He suffered night sweats
and matted nodes. What were the odds
his final scan would come out clear?

I dream about St. Christopher
carrying Corrigan on his shoulders
across the river. Far from the shore,
the compassionate giant pauses,
harried by venomous fish of doubt.
Will the saint continue his trek
toward heaven, or return Corrigan
to the world? Leaning against his staff,
Christopher resigns himself to returning
the man.
            When Corrigan meets me
the next morning, he's dashing to depart.

Irene

After the third stroke,
her words fell off
to a few soft syllables.
When I walk
from behind her wheelchair
to look into red-rimmed eyes
that can't help
looking toward the left,
she cocks her jaw
and her cheekbones swell.
With what looks like weakness,
she wobbles
her left hand to my wrist,
but that grip
is the grip of a woman
who clings by a root
to the face of a cliff.
When she speaks, her words
are small stones
and loosened particles
of meaning
that tumble to their deaths
before my ear
is quick or close enough
to save them. *Irene,*
tell me again, I say,
after the words
in her bits of chopped breath
are gone. But George

takes his cap from my desk
and puts it on his head and says
Doc, her gulps don't make no sense.

Eight Hands

Appendages

I've never been good with them.
My scissoring makes jagged edges.
The sensitivity of my touch
on a vein is dull, followed by
a puncture too deep or too slow.

Like two neurotic children
when they make a mess of a task,
they invent an excuse and say
the stupid project was my idea —
appendages are not to blame.

I've never understood why they
disguise their motivation
from my brain. I imagine
handfuls of accomplishment
but my hands don't agree.

Vaudeville

It's come to this — bowels. Six weeks
from the time you teeter, fall
and spend the night strapped to a gurney,
your hands lie in wait, jump, grab,
tap my fingers. You talk about bowels
but *hey!* Yours are not the hands of misfortune.
They have a life of their own, buds
at the end of old boughs. Your skin hangs
from sickness, fever, fasting,
but not your hands. Your hands put on
an old one-two, a little vaudeville
between the act in which you lose
your brothers, wife and common sense,
and the act where knots are loosened,
pipes reamed out and ropes replaced.
Every morning brings a new task,
a new way of looking at what's left.
Your eyes water like sulfur springs,
your body is pale, tenuous, devoted
to bowels, but your hands quip *Hey Bones!*
dancing that old soft shoe.

Anita and Vladimir

Anita, whose course of radiation
hasn't sprung the tiniest leak
in her character, tells me the blues
that crawl each morning into her bed
are masculine. The icicle jitters
that slip under her skin by evening
are feminine. She gets rid of the men
by belting *What a Friend We Have
in Jesus* until the nurses come
and shush her. She relies on the Spirit
to hustle petulant women
out of the room. Anita's calm.

Vladimir, whose battle with cancerous
marrow has taught him to dissect
the brain's intoxicated tics,
wags a pear-shaped head made shiny
by steroids. I expect him to explain
Anita's deficits — superstition,
dullness, delirium. Last evening
in the family room, he lectured
on chemo to his roommate's daughter
until she turned away.
I'm shaken
when Vladimir kisses Anita's hand.

Hands of Enchantment

This is as far as it goes,
my first girlfriend said
and nodded to the knot
of our clasped hands.

Fifteen, and not even
a kiss. Since then my hands
have navigated a lot
of ground — the cream,

the most enduringly
supple and enchanting
continent of which,
my heaven, is your skin.

The Silk Robe

> "... the white baubles and silk stockings of
> your actresses excite my genitals."
> — Samuel Johnson, on going backstage
> at Drury Theater

There's little excitement under the skin
of these bright halls. Though much of the flesh
is female, it's doughy from blockage
and muddled with wounds. The corridors'
odor — a confusion of solvents, seepage,
and hundreds of intimate chemicals.
Lit from behind by the bathroom light,
your blue silk robe has no place in this picture.
The scent you wear — Samsara, Gardenia,
Chanel? — is alien. When I walk in
your expression is amazed it's morning again
and I've returned to examine
your perfect chest. Perfect, except for
the swishing and rasping endocarditis.
I notice the flowered barrettes in your hair,
the creamy coolness you must have just
put on, your fingers asking me to sit.
Another two weeks, I explain, of bed rest
and intravenous. In here the drama
belongs to others, patients whose stories
twist into bitterness or blossom into gain
before going home. Nothing about you
fits the scene. Not the gauze clutching your groin
where they snaked a catheter up to your heart.
Not your toenails, painted maroon,

nor the delicate gold chain. There's not much
danger now — for you. Your cultures are clean.
You're upright and walking the halls.

The Exterior Palace

Dressed for cocktails at noon, Mrs. Melville
greets me by putting her whiskey down
while raising herself with her quad cane.
My entrance — her nurse's cue to complain
about her patient's tantrums and rejections.
I lean on a lovely couch in the sunroom,
listening to the nurse's soprano line —
still drinking despite strict instructions,
copping smokes, flouting noncompliance.
Below it, a contralto line — *Doctor,*
we've got to get rid of that bitch of a nurse.
Tools of the trade fill my bag, but nothing
will set this ecology right. The nurse,
I suppose, is driven by trust in the power
of words to enlighten and of reason
to sweep the deck. My patient likes to flirt
and kibitz. She believes I'll wink
at her badness. She thinks I'm not
permitted to divulge our secret —
her internal palace, beyond its moat
and portcullis, beyond the magnificent
central court, is a dank, unheated place.
Neither of us goes there. I'm enjoying
a delicate pattern of sunlight
across the rug and six framed photos
of different sizes that show her smiling.

Ascension Thursday

Patients sit by their beds in the Vets ward,
scanning the storm in their windows,
listening to thunder. Renko wears
pale green pajamas for hope. He pulls
a Lucky from the pack under his pillow
and puts a match to its tip, but a tremor
in the tattooed web between his finger
and thumb won't stop. He swivels around
Hook's deserted bed and parks at a window,
anticipating this year his ascension
will happen, despite all the main chances
he has missed in his life. Riffs of thunder
menace the empty stadium below
and the fancy nuthouse on the terrace
below that. A peculiar yellow light
arises within the storm, where the sun
ought to be setting. The breaks until now
have always stayed a step ahead of Renko
but this time he is sure an ascension
will happen. Like a cautious squirrel, his heart
pauses halfway up the trunk, ears perked,
listening for the crack of a dry branch.

Lift Up Your Heart

An ER treatment room at 2 AM.
On a gurney, a mangled body
cops brought in — *resisting*.

Awakened from a stupor, the beast
curses me, straining at straps
across his chest and hips. His vision

bleeding — confusion, fear, loathing.
Muscles at the back of my neck tense,
fingernails scrape across slate.

A package of tools on a tray.
As I begin to stitch the edges
of the man's wound, he twists his head,

spits at my too-close face, a glob
hits my eyebrow; a second, my mask.
No let-up. The cops will soon be back

to process my patient
and put him into the system
he resisted.

If I squeeze a portion of my heart
in a press, will a few drops
of compassion drip into my cup?

Ralph Angelo Attends the Barbeque

At the St. Charles Nursing Home barbeque picnic,
Ralph Angelo, wearing his signature straw hat,
strains his neck toward Gary, the man with a mike
and Hawaiian shirt, who badgers us to clap
to the thrumming boom box on a chair beside him,
chanting, *Heart of my heart   I love that melody.*
Ralph holds a tissue in each hand. He presses one
against the side of his veined nose, the other
to the crease of his mouth to collect his drool.
On Ralph's tray are plastic cups of thickened juice
and pureed hamburger. *Heart of my heart   brings back
a memory.* I feed him. Gary ribs the crowd
for not jumping to dance in the meadow, a joke
that falls flat. When Ralph puts his lips in motion,
they glide like snails across bricks. His puff
of consonants disappears below the drone.
His vowels die off. I kneel and put my ear
near his mouth to listen, but Ralph's lips
resemble a body being pulled toward the ground
while hanging from nails in the entryway.
Embarrassed, I ask Ralph what he means,
but his stony lips, his watery eyes,
fail to disclose, and Gary continues *Oh,
you beautiful girl   You great big beautiful girl.*
Volunteers passing by us distributing ice cream cups
remind me of the frozen chasm between us.

Two of Them

The old Russian couple
in adjoining chairs
teeter toward each other
and tell me everything.

She demonstrates the jolt
at the edge of sleep
by jabbing a finger at me,
vindictively.

He shows his scalp – it crawls
with emptiness at night
and keeps him up. *There,*
he bats it behind his ear.

I think he sold diamonds
for a living, enough
to convince himself, he
said once, *it's not much*

of a life. At the end
of her list is *Need sleep*
underlined twice, and *What
happened to my eyes?*

Take Off Your Clothes

I was taught to include specific
detail, like *down to your underpants
and socks*, or *all but your panties
and bra*, whichever might apply.

And season my request with modest
withdrawal, *I'll step out of the room
for a moment now*. And follow this
with the obvious, *Then I'll come back*.

I was taught always to offer a gown,
frequently folded backwards and faded,
and tell the patient, *Put the opening
behind. Put this sheet across your lap*.

In the next step, I learned to uncover
the roots of bewilderment, beginning
with the eyes and continuing down,
a performance laden with gesture,

encouraging hope. I delivered my script.
And you, my intimate companion,
you were consigned to endure the suspense
of me reading a narrative in your flesh.

Metamorphosis at Starbucks

Knobs appear beneath a drab sweater.
He comes in wearing a dark skirt
and gypsy blouse. When he sits at a table
near me, I notice the scarlet nails.
In a short time, I switch to the pronoun
she prefers. Several mornings a week
we sit, our backs to the windows,
two tables apart. When a story appears
in the *Times* on a marvel of medicine,
she brings it to my attention,
addressing me as *Doctor*. I'm surprised
her voice hasn't softened. Her poise
remains masculine. Her breasts become larger
but her face and arms, though smoother,
reveal the old sharp scaffolding.
With regard to an article
that touts advances in gene therapy,
she becomes flustered at my lack
of enthusiasm. With regard to a piece
about a theatrical new cure
for depression, I suggest reserving
just a pocket of doubt. In the months
that follow, her salt-and-pepper hair
remains dull, her makeup impasto,
her posture graceless. Metamorphosis
has ground to a halt, though trinkets of change
continue to accumulate. Each morning
I look for a difference I can't put my
finger on, but have faith it will shine through

when it happens. I yearn to nudge her,
to tip her toward happiness. She's not
like those miracles in the paper; she's real.

The Rule of Thirds

Third, third, third — the rule I learned
about the stories of the ill.

A third get well — joints begin to move,
pain improves, depression's dull

embrace is eased. The villain leaves
without a trace and no one knows

the hero's name — doctor
or patient, science or grace.

A third grow crippled in the pain
of joints gone stone, their minds decline,

the villain takes the loot no matter what
the dour professor does, or you —

in the arrogance of youth — might try.
We learn by progress in our minds.

A third remain the same. They take
the villain in, they harbor him

until his tale is theirs and theirs is his.
They visualize their bodies with his eyes.

Our rule of thirds was not as kind
as love's compassion is,

nor as thunderous as an essay
on machines, but it spoke

the language of the body
in its genes.

He Lectures at the Heritage Association Dinner

After dessert, the women
arranged themselves upstairs
in a private room. He began
by presenting the usual
distinction between letting
a patient die and killing.
His examples generated
a spark that ignited
tiny firecrackers behind
a dozen faces and waving
hands rose, *Doctor! Doctor!*
A husband suffering torture
long after his body
gave out — a physician's hubris.
An injured brother severed
from machines too soon
by doctors who had stolen
his wife's consent.
Passion took hold of the group.
Anger and urgency tore
great hunks of experience
from the women's hearts
and grief uncovered its roots.
Having sprung the hinges
of ethics, he sampled
the best dose in his cabinet —
silence. When passion subsided,

the president praised the talk
that had not been given
and thanked him profusely
for sharing his wisdom.

The Second Act

My first student with cancer wasn't a star
by any means. He stood out from his class,
missing sixteen of twenty-four questions
on the quiz about cardiac murmurs.
He examined his patient for an hour —
came away with disconnected notes
and no idea. When he didn't show up
after the break, I figured he'd discovered
his mistake, dropped out. February came.
March. On the first of May, he appeared
in my office, greenish, gaunt, and bald.
Fingering an Irish cap, he apologized
for keeping *Wintrobe's Diseases of the Blood*
so long and promised to return it soon.
His eyes, anchored on a plastic Yoda
beside my phone, bobbled to mine
each time he spoke. He had come to terms
with sarcoma. *But I failed the chemo,*
he chuckled, *a little irony, don't you think?*
When he scooted the chair closer,
I couldn't help but see the scapular
of the Sacred Heart, bright green for hope,
hanging beneath his shirt. *I'll come to class
as often as I can,* he said. *And work
to make-up.* My first student with cancer's face
hovered uncomfortably close as he asked,
*Please tell the class the tumor's gone.
I couldn't stand their pity.*

A Long Shot

for John Wright,
oncocytoma, 2450 grams

A burst of unwelcome blood, a painless,
alarming apparition. You figure
the options, a calculus you've practiced

hundreds of times with the lives of others;
now every door you open
and the darkness beyond it is your own.

On the scan a mass the size of a sack
of potatoes sitting atop your kidney,
a tumor Fortune dropped off in her haste

to desert you. Or did she? More devious
than that, she's played a trick. Full stop.
As you quietly turn up your last hand —

the tumor is benign! Fortune tossed a coin
behind her left shoulder when leaving
the room. She must have known you'd catch it.

If she allows you keep that coin for a time,
you'll be set — until she collects the debt.

Livedo Reticularis

In the final stages of shock, his weak,
distended heart and stagnant blood
sketch a map of archipelagos
across his back and buttocks.

Taught that hearing is the last sense
to remain, I say, *Sorry, my friend,*
as I tend his wound. My tampering
tears tissue-paper skin.

That pearl of wisdom about hearing?
I'm skeptical. What was its source?
Those who come back? My finger traces
a route along the rim of his hip.

It might be the angel of death's path
or the wake of a nautical hearse
about to dock. His skin's reddish blotches
are clouds reflected in a calm lagoon —

red sky at morning, sailors take warning.
Scent of Betadine, raft of fresh white gauze
and tape. Silence in the room. A few
wake up before they die. Fewer speak.

Unsettled Weather

The hostile wind is at its worst tonight.
Rain is fierce and thunder jars cement.
Upstairs, a woman who should have died
last week — she did, but medics came —
slips backward and sheds an interior layer,
like the beach of a barrier island
when a hurricane carries it under.

Above the entry wound, my patient's cheek
is swollen purple, her zygomatic arch
turned citrus tense. A sister from Wyandanch
rests her fingers on a hand that's overripe.
No, no, we can never give up. Scars constrict
the patient's lungs from too much care.
The only secret that remains is her.

Skinwalkers

In these old buildings
deaths accumulate.
Though each is transparent,
it leaves behind a taste
of someone, a skinwalker.

In a bustling elevator
I'm surrounded by skinwalkers
who want to assist me.
They look antiseptic
and distracted, like people

doing and touching
the things they remember.
Some sip their coffee and smile.
Some steer their IV poles
like bishops' holy crosiers.

The skinwalkers mumble,
G'morning, when they jostle
and bump me, so closely
their touch is lotion
that clings to my raw hands.

Hardly anyone remembers
the dead can't harm us.
Hardly anyone notices
these faint souls, flickering
with traces of sympathy.

TWO

Burial Rite

Vedbaek, Denmark,
5000 BCE

They decorated her dress with boar's teeth
and tiny shells, smeared her limbs with ochre,
and placed her head on a deerskin pillow.

They put the body of her newborn son
into the crook of her arm and covered him
with the soft, extended wing of a swan.

For protection on the perilous journey
to the land of the dead, they laid
a freshly sculpted flint knife in her hand.

In her leather-like stomach, the remains
of a mother's last meal before giving birth —
seeds of wild plants. Some of them sprout.

Aesculapius Writes His Memoirs

Artemis arsoned my mother —
set her on fire with me
in the womb — for shaming
the Olympians
by marrying a mortal
after Apollo, my father,
had screwed her.
Thank Zeus, he ripped me out
before it was too late.

My father fostered me
to Chiron, the centaur,
who taught me the arts
of magic and healing,
arts I learned so well
that soon I gained the power
to cure Philoctetes' sore,
Achilles' heel, or ancient
Oedipus' blinded eyes,
even Medusa's hair,
even Medea's character.

I wanted more. The lust
for gold and power
consumed me. I crept
closer and closer
to godliness. One day
I crossed the boundary
by reviving a man
whose time had come.
Looking down my nose

at Fate, I brought him back
from Hades' bony grip.

Surely Apollo
would protect me
from the upshot
of hubris — my worst
miscalculation.
Zeus hurled a thunderbolt
that vaporized redeemer
and redeemed alike.
Poof! The underworld
absorbed my patient's
residual vapor.

As for me — Lord Zeus,
despite his philandering
a stickler
for family honor, flinched
from the shame of leaving
his grandson a shade
in hell. Instead,
with what delicious
irony, he created me
the god of healing —
a bum job with few
benefits, many burdens —
eternally pestered,
always on call.

To the Heart of Lazar Riverius, Galenist Physician

Today the surgeons shut you down,
open, patch you, put in plastic —
and not a single Sign of the Cross!

Spirit? They don't try to tackle
the larger problems, the problems
Lazar Riverius posed.

In the old days you opened your arms
in diastole, swelling with welcomes.
In rushed the blood, in came air —

razzamatazz! The humors mixed
and, heart, you created spirit.
Now that was an accomplishment.

Elegant and mysterious,
spirit descended like dew
into a thicket of body parts.

Spirit ascended like steam,
informing Riverius' head
with movement and memory.

Spirit rattled his arteries —
a puppeteer pretending wind —
and souls and bodies blended.

Then scientists cut their cadavers.
Heart, they made an ox of you,
pumping the blood in dispirited circles.

Sts. Cosmas and Damien Perform the
First Human Leg Transplant

Fra Angelico captures Cosmas and Damien
at the moment of attachment. They've placed
the dead Ethiopian's right lower leg
into position. Their patient, a fair-skinned deacon
whose ulcerated leg they amputated,
seems to have ascended to another plane
or passed out. Their next step would have been
to suture the ebony leg to the rosy thigh,
unless holiness served as the adhesive.

Coming out of his swoon, did the deacon
reward his surgeons with a pocketbook
of prayers? Was a period of recovery
required, or did the patient limp home
the same day on his transplanted leg?

The holy surgeons were dangerous men.
They might have survived by offering
a dove to the emperor and paying
the specified fine, rather than martyrdom.
Their persecutors attempted drowning,
stoning, burning, and crucifixion —
all without success. How befuddled
the soldiers must have been! In beheading
the saints they found a sure thing.

McGonigle's Foot

Philadelphia, 1862

McGonigle is dense in thought,
a step beyond his bout with drink.
Filbert Street trips up his back
and turns his ankle from behind.

A foreigner, a drunk, and loud,
the surgeon scratches in his book.
No need to etherize this case.
That night they amputate the foot.

McGonigle is pinned to bed
by rippling arms, his swollen leg
is roped to frame. The surgeon saws
as quick as sex. The leg kerplunks.

Retching, terrified, and screaming,
the Irishman curses the Virgin
and Jesus. *Keep your distance, men,*
the surgeon in his apron warns.

The lower orders of the race
have nerves more coarse than ours,
a boon in light of all the shame
and filth unfortunates endure.

You must use ether wisely, men,
by judging risk against the gain.
The young men shift from foot to foot.
McGonigle goes down for good.

For pain is our Creator's gift
to teach and strengthen us, a most
desirable — though never sought —
companion, men. So, humbly, cut.

Floating Kidney

> "'The kidney, a floating kidney.' He recalled
> all the doctors had told him of how it detached
> itself and swayed about."
> — Tolstoy, *The Death of Ivan Ilych*

1.

A listless organ sailing at random
among foggy ports, slippery tales,
a host of alien customs.

Source of inexplicable symptoms —
lurching stomach, angry groin,
rotating pain of an absent stone.

Unless a surgeon stitches him
to a pier, he floats like the Dutchman,
damaging every life he touches.

2.

My mental kidney is contrary —
he spins yarns of floating freely
where he wishes. Guilty dreams.

Unlike his abdominal brother,
the mental kidney considers
stability a burdensome cross.

My mental kidney imagines
a better life — unmet wishes.
My abdominal kidney pisses.

The Testimony of Mary Clues' Daughter

Oh, how the learned doctors have lied
about Mary Clues! They reckoned that drink
and the soft corpulence of female parts
were at fault. They reckoned a woman
whose liver was grim as her husband's heart
was a freak and her lust for vice was such
that she died of spontaneous combustion.

Yes, I found my mother at half after five
in the morning — a heap of ash with her
smoldering head at one end, the charred clubs
of two feet at the other, her room
painted with soot the color of burnt fat.
A fire that exploded from the grate
had consumed her. Anyone could see that.

But the learned doctors said the grate
had nothing to do with it. They claimed
her female fat embalmed in drink
plus the fetid morals of our class
accounted for her bursting into flame!
Explanation, cause — all those fine words
doctors use to put their ignorance
into a box and hide it. They're not true.

Ma was drunk, that's sure, and she died
in a fire. But the rest of their tale —
spontaneous combustion caused by taint —
is a lie they tell to frighten the poor.
Female bodies are made to be sober
and virtuous, to cook the dinner,
to wash the clothes.

Funny, All I Can Think About Is Sin

On a line by Alphonse Daudet

False spring is making its rounds this morning
in the way my nurses talk, "A lovely wound...
it's wonderful... his leg is pinker." Charming,
you'd think they were talking about flowers.

The way my nurses talk about the wound
is false. My leg's a strip mine all worked out.
What are they talking about? Not flowers.
My wound's a sulfurously layered pit,

undermined, a wrong that won't work out,
an ulcer, which digs deeply into sin,
releasing brimstone vapor from the pit.
How weird is this delirium I'm in?

Funny, all I can think about is sin.
My nurses' pants caress their moving butts.
They're lovely, though this delirium
confuses me. "His wound is wonderful..."

The movement of their pink caressing butts.
I imagine my flowery nurses —
it's confusing — wonderfully wound-up.
They float away, praising my lovely wound.

Then I imagine my flowery nurses
a little later, as the morphine wears off
and they float back, not praising my lovely wounded
leg, but raucously laughing, like kookaburras.

Later, when my morphine wears away,
there'll be no false spring on morning rounds,
but raucous kookaburras will echo
wonderfully, "Charming and pink, charming and pink."

Icon of the Heavenly Ladder of St. John Klimakos

St. Catherine Monastery,
Sinai, 12th Century

The heavenly ladder rises from lower left
to upper right corner where the Lord beckons
from the gate of heaven, a curved opening
on the golden horizon. The blessed figure
welcomes the pure of heart
who ascend the ladder, eyes lifted in rapture.
The others climb precariously, threatened
at every step by miserable dark angels
harassing them with prods and lassos.

Of the twenty-six figures, only seven
have fallen to perdition, not a bad
proportion. In the upper left-hand corner,
an angelic choir observes the climbing chain
and its weakening links. Given their own
perfection, these beings seem puzzled
by conflicted motivation.

Below the ladder on the right, the damned
huddle inside a hill, encased in amber.
They wear the same robes and sober beards
their fellows do. They elevate their arms
in prayer. One reaches to the very rim
of damnation, his finger nearly poking
into heaven, seeking compassion.

THREE

Phone Call from Alaska

for Heather

That you were shot. That it was only a flesh wound
in your left upper arm. That it came through the window
above the sink in your basement apartment.
A pop. A pin. That you had no idea what it was until
a burn below your shoulder, glass shards in the sink.
Straight through your meat. It's nothing serious,
you insist. Again.

I have to imagine your teapot whistling.
Your oatmeal. Your pieces of peanut butter toast.
I have to imagine it all. Not a sniper,
but a kid getting a jump on Halloween morning.
A trick, but no treat. A scare, but no harm, you repeat
for the fifth time.

Twenty-two caliber. That they found the bullet
on the kitchen floor under the table near your boots.
That you drove to the ER, took the rest
of the day off work. That it was meaningless, random,
so to speak, you chuckled, shot in the dark,
but it made you think.

Appetite

In the belly of Port Jefferson ferry
a biker varooms his bellowing engine
while I think of Marcus Aurelius
who wrote, *Wipe out the imagination.*
A signal for the other leather jackets
to start their bikes. A warning to anyone
who thinks these tough specimens of fifty
will obey the rules. I wait in my neat
suburban wagon for the ferry's nose
to open.

They stood at the bar the whole crossing
stretching black jackets and boasting
about whose cycle was the cat's ass
and whose city Atlantic was. One woman
with *Steel Pier* spelled in stars on the back
of her jacket said, *Fucking desire,*
again and again while I waited in line
for a beer. There must be twenty bikers
making salt air sour with fumes down here,
varooming! their hearts to a standstill.

Fucking desire. I wonder if Aurelius
was in Rome, or living in a tent
on some campaign, when he wrote about
contentment. Bikers will speed the grade
from Port Jefferson and fly the spine
of Long Island like a line of tough crows.
I buy gas and go home, imagining
the bones in that woman's face
when she said, *Fucking desire,* remembering
the Emperor Aurelius who wrote, *Wipe out
imagination. Check desire. Extinguish
appetite.*

War Remnants Museum, Ho Chi Minh City

The bulk of the remnants are photographs
of crimes — a naked girl whose skin is on fire
from splotches of napalm, a vacant hillside
with dead trunks, relics of Agent Orange.

Larger remnants sit on the grounds outside —
an American Chinook aircraft,
a Russian-built tank, a fragment of sewer
from Thanh Phong in which three children hid.

Some remnants have sprung into being
since then — In carts and wheelchairs and braces
at the building's entrance, a chorus
of song-filled children, playing instruments

with toes and prostheses, living remnants
of hubris, as is the ingot of shame
in my heart. During the applause, they smile
at the audience and nod their heads.

Christmas in Kosovo

Some of the bodies were scattered on a hill
above the road. The others were heaped
in a gully. Most of them had their eyes
gouged out, including a 12-year-old boy
the police said was a hardened terrorist.
One of the men was found in the courtyard,
decapitated, and so far his head
remains missing. Many had been shot
at close range, after the soldiers pricked them
with machetes and brass knuckles. Later,
the women were raped, and in some cases
their bones were broken. The one woman
we talked to was cut across both sides
of her face. Reporters said it's the worst
threat we've had in months to the process
of peace, which they assured us is fragile —
unlike women's wails as they returned
from the evacuation and discovered
eyeless corpses. We counted the bodies.
We noted their positions, the nature
of their wounds, and the extent to which
their condition reflected abomination.
This, a week or so after the Prince of Peace
had come to Europe, an interval in which
the fabric of the world was drenched in hope.
Meanwhile, the leader of the peacekeepers
rummaged in his bucket of language
to find a message for the viewers.
This was done, he told them earnestly,
by those who place little value on human life.

To the Mummy of a Thief in the
Crypt of St. Michan's Church, Dublin

After six hundred years, the watery parts
are gone — intestines, muscle, liver, spleen.
Your lizard-like surface has turned turf brown.
Yet the wages of your sin remain —
stumped bones instead of hands, your single foot.
A thief, hung at last for your fourth offense.
We don't know why he's here, the sexton says,
interred with saints. In the slot above you,
the pickled body of a knight carried
home from the Holy Land, whose crossed arms
embrace an absent sword. His last Crusade.
And lying stiffly in the dust beside you
is a 14th century nun. She whose body
Christ once warmed with grace now lies snug
against your sacrilegious arm. Your tale
is told in severed bones, but hers is gone.
Her cloister's stone is cobbled in the streets
of Dublin. *Some say it's chemicals that makes
these bodies mummify, something in the ground
like gas.* The sexton shakes his head. *Some say,
it's grace. St. Michan's gift. A kind of miracle.
Who knows?* He points us toward the steps.
Your head is propped between two bricks, its eyes
are talking to the nun. Does she believe
the tale you tell — I begged for bread, I stole to live?
Judge for yourself, the sexton says and slams
and bolts the heavy door. *I think it's gas.*

At the Egyptian Market in Istanbul

Pomegranates. Sacks of spice. Garish dolls
with battery-powered hips gyrate on a crate
covered with carpets. What infernal heat!

A folding table with an oversized jar.
In its murky water, hundreds of leeches,
clumps of them, cling to the greenish glass.

A somnolent man in a tent-like garment
sits beside the sign — ARTHRITIS (in English).
BLOOD CLOT. SWELLING. VARICOSE VEIN.

A small boy slips behind the table
and dips his hand into the leeches'
container. The vendor swears and swats him.

Leeches wave like kelp in a dirty tide.
The blood-sucking monsters thrive in the heat.
Gyrating belly dancers slow down and stop.

Montazah Gardens, Alexandria

On the corniche a brightly colored knot
of children begs an American woman
to repeat their names — Habibah, Neema,
Husani, Ife. Smiling pink scarves

push closer. An impish boy asks her,
*Do you live in a mansion? Can I come
to New York?* Behind them, the bay's
flat arms open, and on the horizon

sit scribbles of the distant city,
concealing its squalor and violence.
Among the orange and azure robes
and giggling girls, one wearing a burka

stands a head taller than the others.
As I place a frame around these children,
much like the city frames the park and the park
its lovers, she raises her hands, palms out,

thumbs together, toward the camera,
as if to frame her invisible face —
or photograph me. Through the slit, the bridge
of her nose appears, her luminous eyes.

Fish Massage

Siem Reap, Cambodia

I slip off my clogs and submerge my feet
in the fish tank for relief
of my migraine, muscle ache, fatigue, and stress.

Two clouds of tiny fish nibble my soles
for their sloughed cells, sweat, and dirt,
debris that pins me down.

I sip the cup of Cambodian beer
free with each treatment, but refuse
to purchase a sacred penis.

At the next tank, two Filipino girls
squirm with delight, *It tickles!*
while a third videos their feet.

Ignoring the parasites in the water,
I chuckle, seduced
by such unwholesomeness.

Night Vision

Uluru, Australia

Above the black desert
a bewilderment of pinpricks
shines. A pair of red twins.

Antares, a ball of gas
nearly the size
of the orbit of Jupiter.

The arid planet Mars,
a residue of rock
tortured by blasts of dust.

Boiling furnace, tiny speck.
One emits, one reflects.
Past progressive, present tense.

One's distance measured in time,
one's size in distance,
like my heart's attachments —

some stare, others twinkle.

"Pair Chase Boy for His Urine"

Tucson Daily Courier
October 28, 1998

Five bucks to piss in a cup, no strings attached,
says the man in a muscle shirt. He seems sincere.
Raunchy, but it's a solid plan he's hatched.

The woman with a dirty scarf. They're matched,
like two cracked cups. Nothing there to fear.
Five bucks to piss in a cup, no strings attached.

Just step behind the bushes — job dispatched.
The two of them are desperate to appear
squeaky clean. It's a solid plan they've hatched.

Lanky hair, sallow skin, their faces splotched
with hopefulness. I wonder if it's fair.
Five bucks to piss in a cup, no strings attached.

A dirty specimen — they'll both be scratched
from rehab in a snap. So much for their
second chance. It's a solid plan they've hatched.

Should I do it? Or should I be detached
and tell the cops? Or just get out of here?
Five bucks to piss in a cup, no strings attached.
I'll ask for more. A solid plan they've hatched.

Deliver Us From Evil

for Al Clah

You stride the arroyo to the clinic
in Greasewood, coldly sober,
carrying your battered portfolio.
You rage about the pinto horse
that died last night in your corral,
the dream that woke your nephew
in a sweat — a wolf became a man.

You talk of corpse dust sprinkled in
your sister's camp, the need to hire
a holy man with power enough
to end an enemy's curse. So I buy
an awkward landscape from your folder —
in the distance sandstone buttes,
horses drinking from a desert pool.

Where once you added shadow
to the pool (its source I couldn't guess),
paleness bordered by a pencil line
remains. After forty years the buttes
have faded to yellow, the horses
ghostly tan, their color vacuumed
back to the past, like ardor and angst.

The painting is not a landscape
with horses. Its subject is fading,
the paling of diminishment and time.
Disappearances occur. The wolfman
recedes in his appearances, until
evil is nothing but ordinary
and your horse, my friend, just dead.

Sacrament of the Sick

Limpopo Province

What if Flora came back, not made of sticks
and sinews creeping across the room
on Granny's arm, but in a bright blue robe
with shimmering yellow lines and a dozen
jangling bracelets, and the cardboard coverings
of her windows turned to glass, and the bent
aluminum fork her daughter is digging
in the dirt with became a doll dressed in glitter
and sequins. What if Flora could ambush
the Minister of Health at the point of a knife
and imprisoned her in an underground chamber,
where she would tie the Minister's tongue
and stick a tube in her throat and siphon out
the Minister's moisture, until she was dry
as a mummy from the Kalahari.
What if Flora came back, not struggling
toward her bed in muslin, but wearing
a brash Sotho blanket and crimson turban,
dancing *Morena boloka setjhaba*.
What if, after Benedict anointed her
with oil and chrism and made the sign
of the cross on her lips, Flora could pour
protein and lemon juice and garlic bits
into the Minister's throat until her skin
shimmered with life, and Flora forgave
her cruelty and lies. What if everything

were different, and Flora's daughter
didn't die, and Flora's husband
kept his pants buttoned. What if Benedict's
blessing ascended to God, like a comet
skidding from here to the Ort cloud.

Cesium 137

Goiania, Brazil

"... an old radiotherapy source
was taken from an abandoned
hospital site...."

In a field scattered with axles, fenders,
sets of steel wheels, whole bodies of cars,
children discover the marvelous powder.
At twilight they return with their friends
to revel in its phosphorescence.

One child smears cesium on his arms
and climbs beneath an abandoned car
to augment his glow. His sister makes rouge
of the powder on her cheeks and tastes
the miraculous stuff. Others shove dabs
into their pockets and plastic purses.

This is the treasure they had hoped
to discover, the cairn of their small lives
burst open — beyond their parents' drab
existence, their loveliness aglow at last.

The children begin to die within the day.
Heads smoldering, mucosa raw,
their bodies vacillate and weaken
hour by hour, consumed by innocence
and radiant desire.

Shall Inherit

Pale as clay they come to school
in Pineville, Kentucky,
carrying the cardboard cups
we gave them, as directed, full,
wrapped in newspapers and bags
with rubber bands in both directions.
They march to teacher's desk,
watching the wall of crayoned squirrels
instead of us, and drop their cups.

The children — gaunt as parents are,
tight as vines, and bred from one
tough root — march barefoot
through these hills until they reach
the porch of Redbird Mission School
and put on shoes. The rat-tat-tat
of shoes on polished boards
wakes me to the work ahead —
spin and fix, stain the cysts.

I watch those sinewy children
with the sweet queerness of ether
in my mind, and hear formaldehyde's
weird voice say *Ascaris*
and innocence. One child has tapeworm,
one child has hook. With their small
serious eyes like coals, they come
on clay roads to Redbird Mission School
wearing the shrunken heads
of ancestors on their shoulders.

Los Locos

Just when the night is stone dry,
the drunks appear, jabbering
a mile a minute in Mexican,
banging my desk with shots
of tequila, smack, smack,
and tossing them back.
Just when I read the page
of discouragement,
my grandfather steps
out of the group
and wafts me a kiss.
Just when I'm famished
from thirst in the desert,
his compadres strum
their vihuelas, winking
like lechers. Grandfather
grabs his crotch and hops
like he's riding a horse.
A wild horse. He grins and sucks
that old yellow tooth of his —
his Fountain of Youth — and hollers
in Mexican, *Muchacho,*
kindness is wiser than truth.

At the Oregon Shakespeare Festival

A small scene inserts itself —
we sit at a coffee bar
in Ashland, Oregon, when God appears
wearing bangles and sweatpants
with a clipboard clutched against her breast,
haranguing us. No more a still small voice
from a crevice. Tomorrow at half past noon
she intends to destroy the city,
indiscriminately. Our final chance
is to depart tonight. God's pudgy face
is neither kind nor angry. Only urgent.
Her mandate — beyond justice or mercy.
Today, her cup of compassion is empty.
My cup is sugarless, black; yours, a skinny,
double shot latte. Lukewarm. Our discussion
regarding religious rituals of forgiveness
loses steam. Without pausing to acknowledge
our questions, God moves to announce
her message elsewhere. End of scene.

FOUR

Out of Ireland

Martin Coulehan
1831-1902

Martin carries a tin chest to the coast
during the worst year of famine, alone.
He must be the son the family can spare —
the youngest, or the one whose crime
or act of shame has put a premium
on fleeing. Perhaps he plans to earn
a passage for his parents when he arrives
in the golden land, yet he reappears
married with a farm in western Maryland,
a faded entry on a census form,
but beyond that, illiterate and mute.

To find a link, I cross the Atlantic.
Public documents destroyed in Dublin
during the uprising. Baptismal records
burnt in the fire of eighteen ninety
at a church along the Shannon River.
A scattering of gravestones eroded
and broken. No surnames. No memory.
At my journey's end, a distracted priest
driving a lawnmower repeats my name
with moist lips. His stained, sweaty cassock,
his thinning hair, the angel at Jesus' grave —
The man you are looking for is not here.

March of Dimes Girl, 1954

She should've been dead,
but the March of Dimes
put her in a kind of
cylinder and saved her.

How long must I wait in line
at the Kansas State Fair
to get a glimpse
of her masterpiece body?

How long must I sweat
in the heat before I slip
through the flaps
of the March of Dimes tent?

Her ivory face hangs out
at the end of an iron lung.
A nurse in a white cape
wipes sweat from it.

Listening to the suck
of her mechanical breath,
I thank the Good Lord
for making Ella Mae Webb,

who must have suffered
more than enough
for the rest of us,
a work to be proud of.

Dr. Barrone

The first time Doctor Barrone came
to my home, I lay on the sofa
drenched in fever, shivering with fear.
Barrone smelled like a monsignor
smoking a cigar. His nose and mustache
hovered maliciously above me
and sprayed. He poked at my stomach.
He toyed with my ears. Just as his paws
were poised to tighten their grip around my neck,
Barrone pulled them back and burst
into his wicked leer. My mother,
God bless her, was convinced that he cared.
From a jar in his bag, he stuffed
a packet with the pills that turned my teeth
yellow, a remnant of that encounter
that still colors me. My mother
smothered the tablets in applesauce
and insisted I eat the poison,
until I picked up my pallet and walked.

Family History

On Sundays before dinner,
Aunt Mary, whose breast hadn't
turned cancerous yet, insisted
I climb to my grandmother's room.
In the stairwell, carnivorous vines
that grew in the wallpaper
between rows of bloodstained daggers
terrified me. The old woman's
camphorous sick room smothered
the glow from her bedside lamp
as I walked in. In a lumpy
yellow voice, she demanded
I step closer and put my lips
to her forehead. After dinner,
the aunts propped up her body
with pillows. We circled the bed
and recited the Five Sorrowful
Mysteries of the Rosary.
Beneath her repulsiveness, I felt
a dark current — whispers
and glances, my father's night trip
to Chicago for Laetrile,
tense arguments in the kitchen.
I couldn't help wondering
in which of the mansions
God made for the righteous in heaven
would my grandmother live?

Fever of Unknown Origin

Nothing to put my finger on, nowhere
to hang a hat, my illness is evident,
its source in doubt. Its possible causes,
a Scheherazade of stories —

Since coming back from another
continent, I carry a secret wound.
Or: my incorrigible thymus
sizzles in the grease of its own mistake.

Or: a tumor has taken to a cavern
in my deepest layer. The enemy
has slyly disguised its aggression
and tricked me. I hold to an old script

that says calamities have reasons,
the body's machinery is
transparent, and determination
discovers truth. Convenient nonsense,

but sometimes true. My temperature
may drop, despite its firm grip.
I may yet get drunk on bubbles of hope.

Role Model

A hairy man with eyebrows
as thick as Ernie Kovacs'
kneaded my upper back
and murmured in his
hypnotic voice, *Relax,*
let your muscles soften,
while prone on his table
I tightened at the scent
of gardenias he exuded.
The doctor dug his thumbs
into my spine, humming
like an humongous dwarf,
an entity far beyond
what I, at fifteen, had
ever known. He told me
migraines were messages
from my body, spoken
in a language I could learn
if I was sharp. *Sit up,* he said,
and listen. The first lesson:
my profusion of hormones
was natural, a state
without shame. Second:
no masturbation. It would
weaken my system. Third:
work out. And fourth: avoid
entanglement with girls.
Is that all? Messages
an assistant priest had taken
the boys aside last year
to give. I wanted a pill

for my headaches. I wanted
to get out of his office
and take a shower, to hide
my shame in a book. A vague
craving began to unfold,
a thirst to prove the quack
completely wrong, to master
my own medicine.

A Narrow Escape

Sleep paralysis,
the old hag

The old hag enters my room,
wearing a threadbare overcoat
and woolen cap. Shocked from sleep
I struggle to sit, but my bones
are flattened lead tubes, my lips
stitched and drawn tight. The leg
that touches my wife's back, numb.

The hag sits down on my chest,
my ribs collapse, my lungs retract
to fists. In the paralysis
of dying, I panic — a death
without enlightenment. *Clunk,*
clunk — the radiator shutters,
the furnace kicks in, a beam

of light ripples on closed drapes,
water pipes rise in a circus
of farting. At the moment
of crushing, I sense a twitch —
the hag has vanished.
My hand regains its cunning.

Sunday Dinner

"Dog" you know is "God" spelled backwards,
announced my mother, while pouring a can
of baked beans into a bowl beneath her chair
at the table. Hot dogs, mustard, and tuna
for the rest of us around a centerpiece
of sugary green leaf candies. On the surface
her face hadn't changed — a mole on her chin,
a starburst of nasal veins — but her power
had drifted away, leaving a dried residue.
Dad had taken to spending what remained
of his retirement money — a Chrysler
for her to brag about, but she had forgotten
the car was an icon for big shots;
a trip to Spain, where Franco had the trains
on schedule. Like Spain, my father said,
we need to tackle trouble with a firm arm.
His arm reached out to squeeze her shoulder
when she sat. The beagle had already
licked his beans from the bowl by the time
we joined hands and I said the blessing.

The Rock

If any place was safe to discuss
the rock at the nape of my neck,
it was Doctor Werner's office
at his anonymous address
on Bellefield, a brick house
with a porch and double buzzer.
The steps to the second floor
had sealed lips. The flow was such
that one patient walked out
the back before the next
came in. So my muscle-bound
boulder was secure.
Each morning I lifted it
as ballast, a composite
mineral made of my boss,
bad breaks, and fear of failure —
or so I thought. The doctor,
in his cautious Austrian
mumble, suggested I
had misconstrued the rock —
perhaps it consisted, he said,
of fear of success. Success?
The life I'd broken my back
to get? How could I
have sabotaged myself?
Sixteen weeks, sixteen
imperious glances
toward the clock, until my
insurance ran out — we

had to part. I escaped the pain
of chiseling to the core,
my rock as heavy, but less sore.

The Ghost

The ghosts that haunted the mill
hid behind stacks of steel coils and bins
of broken equipment. They clocked in
and curled up to sleep, or stretched out
on benches. Buddies kept a close watch
for a roaming superintendent's hat
where it didn't belong, or a man too green
to keep quiet. Sometimes Dwayne
would wake up in the middle of his shift
at the sindering plant and start
shoveling iron ore onto the belt,
until Brick took his arm and led the frail,
tremulous figure, beholden to bad dreams
and damaged organs, back to his lair.
He's got yellowing of the liver, kid,
and keep your mouth shut. Near the end
when he vomited blood, and they kept him
in the hospital for good, Brick hawked
his plug into a can and told me,
Fuckin' Korea, kid.

Poem for David

The day you died your sheepish letter came
begging me to write Dilaudid for the pain.
On flying home — your goddamn migraines
had come again. After the second bleed
your mother was as good as dead, your dad
a wreck. You begged me to forgive your sick
activities last year, frightening my kids,
bringing meth into my home. *I'm clean,*
you wrote, *Rehabbed in the Vets for months.*

Your drowning made the local Evening News —
a body bobbing at the rocks a quarter mile
beyond the rapids. Swimming when a seizure
took him. An accident, they said. But no.
You hated water, had never learned to swim.
Heroin, Dilaudid, meth. Your manic flight
to help the victims of explosions, earthquakes,
fires — your merciless adrenalin.
Chaos and emptiness tracked you home.

In our Appalachian town, I stood like wax
beside your open casket. Above you —
an arrangement of roses from a woman
named Terri. I hovered near the guttered flame
your father had become, recalling the months
you spent tending the wounded in Vietnam,
your endless shifts in hospitals back home.
I pictured forgiveness — an orchard
carpeted with apples, bruised and fallen.

Revision

Hovering in the normal range
for nearly a year on Paxil,
plumped up, but hardly about
to complain, except for the jazz
of sex, a sense so muted now
and on the curvy side, instead
of spiked. On driving the streets
of the city, the gears I used to
spit stay put, and I don't sputter,
Son of a bitch! by rote. My wife
confessed she'd cringed in her bones
when I used to be erratic
and slip into silent funks.
Now, no more of that — except
after dinner I doze on the sofa
like an undershirt man, watching
an hour of Special Victims Unit
instead of self-improvement.
I feel more than ever like myself,
a feeling that can hardly be true
after sixty years of prowling
outside the fence with the gates
locked or scarier still, open,
swinging, and I would stand there
paralyzed, afraid to step in,
my feet starved for affection
and serotonin shooting itself
in the foot each time a foot perked up
and started to dance. But that can

hardly be true, the way I feel today,
so vividly myself, so *grounded,*
you might say the first draft is done.
I'm in the process of revision.

The Biopsy Room: Prostate

Each punch of the device
thuds in my boggy brain
a fraction of a second
after its teeth bite
a sliver of prostate —
a miniature dragon
attacks my rectum,
a white-clad assistant
slips fragments of tissue
into labeled containers.
Twelve punches, a dozen
vicious bites, the twelve
great labors of Hercules,
especially his capture
of Cerberus, three-headed
sentry of the underworld,
the twelve apostles of Christ,
especially the last, Jude,
patron of impossible
causes, the twelve Knights
of Camelot, especially
Gawain, the purest of heart
who lopped off the head
of the Green Knight,
but found forgiveness,
the twelve Olympian gods,
especially Apollo,
my protector, the zodiac's
twelve constellations,

including Libra, which
augurs balance and grace —
The last punch reminds me
of Cancer, its sharp pincers
won't let go.

"Five Years Ago You'd Be Dead"

My doctor rides on the shoulders
of magnets and molecules, perched
like a Hindu prince on an elephant,
secure in believing my malicious
invader, fatal then, will now succumb
to reason. His confidence predicting
the past unnerves me. Should I be
overjoyed to learn how accidental
my fragile thread's endurance is?
These days, he tells me, the tumor
is hardly worse than a winter cold,
a week of summer insomnia,
or a busted spark plug. I'd like to slip
the illusion into my breast pocket
and keep it close for ten years.

"There's a Time Bomb in Your Chest"

On the way to your office, my body
thrummed basso continuo below
competing fragments and motifs
of consciousness. Some dissonant,
some sweet — each theme comfortably
mine. My organs contributed nothing.
My pancreas, silent. My spleen, mute.
Body parts played pantomime behind
my back, until I discovered
a time bomb was ticking in my chest.

Normality went up in smoke
at the thought the device might trip
at any minute. How could treachery
like this have taken place inside?
Should I have listened more carefully
to the contrabassoon? No telling
the second it's set for, or
how stable its components. My dread
is deafening. *They often erupt*
without warning, you repeat,
swiveling to study the report.

The Queen of Sweden

The transport girl, Garbo as a kid
with acne, backs my wheel chair
through an open elevator door.

I sit with belongings on my lap,
as she patters about the photos
she found in her mother's things

after the funeral. *My grandfather,*
she bursts, *was a cook for the queen*
of Sweden. Seventeen floors

without stopping. Doors open. *One day*
when I marry, she confides, *I'll*
have money and visit the palace.

Like Stockholm, the lobby bustles
with iPhones and roses. White coats
carry cards of survival for some

and scripts that call for the death
of others. My Garbo fidgets
her fingernails between necessity

and hope, transfixed by palaces
of desire. Half here and half there,
weakened, I await the car.

Ockham's Razor

Ockham's razor shaves
stories to their cores,
a stainless blade relieves
complexity — and cures.

I want to say *zebra*,
the razor makes it *horse*.
I imagine a plethora,
am urged a single course.

Simplicity makes sense.
Discarding underbrush,
the secret of success —
a secret, too, of loss.

My rogue imagination
colors, enhances.
My ear yearns to listen,
my thalamus dances.

Now, Ockham's razor sits
no longer trusted
in my medicine cabinet,
abandoned and rusted.

Walt Whitman Reflects on His Doctor's
Bedside Manner

As an old rat that must be allowed to die
in his own way, I start with a prejudice
against doctors. *Never mind worrying*

about your sickness, he scolds me,
I'm seeing to all that. The man tinkers
with platitudes and conceals his thoughts.

In his gospel of encouragement
I'm supposed to be agreeable and dumb
while he puts the best construction

on what's happening. What does he know
about Whitman, the old rat? A shoemaker
tells his customer the shoe fits just right

but the shoe pinches the fellow wearing it.

Retrospective

Forty years passed. His body replaced
its cells, with the exception of his heart's
persistent pump and the mushroom-like paste
of his brain. Only scattered synaptic charts
of his internship remain, etched in myelin,
a few of them deeply. Nonetheless, a dried
umbilical cord connects that powerful womb
to the aging man, across a gulf as wide
as imagination. He doubts there's a thread
to follow, a blockaded door to open,
or a fusty corridor down which to tread
to a solution: those he hurt, the woman
he killed with morphine, more than a few
he saved. His ally, hope, will have to do.

Notes

Burial Rite — In a Mesolithic cemetery near Vedbaek, Denmark, a mother and newborn baby were discovered buried together in a single grave. The child was covered by the open wing of a swan. The cemetery dates from the Ertebølle culture (5300 BCE-3950 BCE).

Aesculapius Writes His Memoirs — Aesculapius, the great physician and future god of medicine, was the son of Apollo and Coronis, a human woman who was subsequently killed by Artemis for falling in love with a mortal man. According to the poet Pindar, Aesculapius was struck dead by Zeus as a result of his hubris in healing a man whom the Fates had decreed should die. Later, Zeus relented and deified Aesculapius.

To the Heart of Lazar Riverius, Galenist Physician — Lazar Riverius (1589-1655) was a French physician and professor at the University of Montpelier. He subscribed to the Galenic theory that venous and arterial blood circulations were separate. Venous blood was created in the liver. Some of it went to the heart, where it mixed with air and "vital spirit" to create arterial blood, which fed the other organs. Thus, the heart was literally the source of spirit.

St. Cosmas and Damien Perform the First Human Leg Transplant — According to Christian tradition, Cosmas and Damian were twin brothers who lived in Cilicia during the late 3rd century. As physicians, they provided free care to the sick. In 287 CE they were martyred for their Christian faith, although their executioners had to try several methods to finally kill them. When one of their white converts lost his leg, they were said to have successfully replaced it with the leg of a recently deceased Ethiopian man.

McGonigle's Foot — Prior to the availability of anesthesia, surgeons depended on opiates and alcohol to quiet their patients and strong assistants to hold them still during surgery. When ether became widely available in the late 1840s, surgeons believed it should only be used selectively, e. g. on patients with "sensibility." This included the educated middle and upper classes. Poor or uneducated patients were thought to have grosser, less sensitive nervous systems and, therefore, did not need to be anesthetized for an operation.

The Testimony of Mary Clues' Daughter — Mary Clues was an elderly woman in Coventry, England, who apparently died of "spontaneous combustion" on the night of March 1, 1772. Her body, reduced to ash except for her legs, was found beside her bed. The room itself had little or no fire damage. The doctor concluded that "her solids and fluids were rendered inflammable, by the immense quantity of spirituous liquors she had drunk." At the time the phenomenon of spontaneous combustion was generally attributed to poverty, drunkenness, and immorality.

Funny, All I Can Think About Is Sin — This poem was inspired by a line from a notebook kept by the writer Alphonse Daudet (1840-1897) recounting his progressive pain and disability from tabes dorsalis, a tertiary form of syphilis. His notes were translated and edited by Julian Barnes under the title *In the Land of Pain* (Alfred A. Knopf, 2002)

Icon of the Heavenly Ladder of St. John Klimakos — St. John Klimakos was a 7th century monk at the Holy Monastery of St. Catherine in Sinai who wrote *The Ladder of Divine Ascent,* which describes the path to spiritual perfection. The icon of the Heavenly Ladder is a 12th century image of the ladder, showing monks climbing toward heaven and devils prodding them (successfully in some cases) to fall into hell.

War Remnants Museum, Ho Chi Minh City — This museum was originally called "Exhibition House for U. S. and Puppet Crimes." Its name was changed to War Remnants Museum in 1995 after the normalization of diplomatic relations between the U. S. and Vietnam.

Sacrament of the Sick — Dr. Manto Tshabalala-Msimang was the South African Minister of Health during much of President Thabo Mbeki's administration (1999-2008). Like Mbeki, she publically expressed doubts that AIDS was caused by the HIV virus and advocated beetroot, garlic, lemons, beer, and African potatoes as treatment for the disease, rather than anti-retroviral drugs. As a result, AIDS medications were not available in South African public hospitals during her tenure.

Cesium 137 — In 1987, at Goiania, Brazil, scavenging children discovered a radiotherapy device that had been left behind in an abandoned hospital. They removed it from the premises and were delighted with phosphorescence produced by a capsule of highly radioactive cesium 137 they discovered inside the device. Twenty children and adults developed radiation sickness and several died.

A Narrow Escape — Folktales from Newfoundland tell of an Old Hag who enters the room and hovers over your bed during the night. You are paralyzed. She descends and sits on your chest, causing a sensation of suffocation. This phenomenon appears under various names in different cultures throughout the world. Medical scientists call it (prosaically) sleep paralysis.

Ockham's Razor – The principle of parsimony articulated most famously by the Scholastic philosopher

William of Ockham (c. 1287-1347): *Entia non sunt multiplicanda praeter necessitatem* (entities must not be multiplied beyond necessity). In medicine this is generally taken to mean that when a patient has multiple symptoms and physical abnormalities, one should look for a single disease that explains them all; and if a common disease accounts for the full syndrome, one should not postulate a rare disease instead.

About the Author

 Jack Coulehan is a poet, physician, and medical educator whose work appears frequently in medical journals and literary magazines. He is the author of five previous collections of poetry, including most recently *Bursting with Danger and Music* (Plain View Press, 2012), and editor of two anthologies, *Blood & Bone* and *Primary Care* (University of Iowa Press, 1998 and 2006). In 2012 he received the Nicholas Davies Award of the American College of Physicians for "outstanding lifetime contributions to the humanities in medicine."

Previous Works by
JB Stillwater Publishing Company

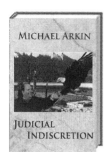

Judicial Indiscretion

Michael Arkin
ISBN: 978-1-937240-63-9
Genre: Judicial Thriller
328 Pages
Available in paperback and eBook
Price: $16.95 paperback, $5.99 eBook

When a local attorney in Mimbres, New Mexico, is indicted and charged with murder of a Judge, Pulitzer Prize winning investigative reporter Linda Lawson of The San Diego Times, enlists Matt Lucas to assist in the defense. Matt, an experienced attorney turned investigator recently relocated from Northern California collaborates with the local Public Defender. Lucas discovers that a banker and The Matranga Cartel may be connected. While investigating, Sheriff Fred Baca and Lucas are almost killed by a Cartel hit squad in Juarez, Mexico. Lucas escapes harm when his home becomes the target of a new hit attempt.

J.W. Valentine

Barbara Novack
ISBN: 978-1-937240-57-8
Genre: Young Adult/Coming of Age
318 Pages
Available in paperback and eBook
Price: $15.95 paperback, $5.99 eBook

Summer 1952, and fourteen-year-old J.W. Valentine wishes the world and everyone in it would leave him alone. His life so far has not gone well. His defenses – anger and cleverness – have only gotten him in trouble. And now the state has sent him to a farm for rehabilitation, something he is determined to resist. He finds in the nearby town resentment and suspicion and, out on the farm, Mac, a man who may know something of value, and Cassie, the girl who will haunt him for the rest of his life. Amid the distrust, there is discovery, and through it, *J.W. Valentine* tells a moving story of love.

Grabbing the Apple
Editors: Terri Muuss and M.J. Tenerelli
ISBN: 978-1-937240-70-7
Genre: Poetry Anthology
114 Pages
Available in paperback
Price: $13.95

The story of Eve has been, more often than not, interpreted by men. Eve has been presented as impulsive, disobedient and ignorant. Where would we be had she never looked for knowledge, asked the important questions, challenged the powers that be? In this beautiful collection of over 40 New York women poets, the strength, vitality and unique voices of women emerge to answer some of these questions. The women whose work has been anthologized in this collection are as bold as New York, as brave as Eve. *Grabbing the Apple* is a powerful an amazing resource for any reader or student who wants to explore an in-depth selection of work from some of New York's finest and strongest women poets.

All I Can Gather & Give
Patti Tana
ISBN: 978-1-937240-45-5
Genre: Poetry
114 Pages
Available in paperback and eBook
Price: $13.95 paperback, $5.99 eBook

All I Can Gather & Give is a book of seventy-five poems by Patti Tana that is composed of three sections: "The Ally You Have Chosen," "Imperfect Circles," and "Every Season Has Its Beauty." This ninth collection of poems is a tribute to the poet's sources of inspiration in nature and the people she loves. In a voice intimate and accessible, Tana finds words to transcend adversity and affirm a life that is passionately lived.

Over Exposed
Terri Muuss
ISBN: 978-1-937240-23-3
Genre: Poetry
136 Pages
Available in paperback and eBook
Price: $13.95 paperback, $5.99 eBook

Muuss brings us close to what we might describe as the secret war, the intimate war, which resides in closed rooms, in seemingly ordinary homes. Yet these poems are written, reader, with such delicacy, such concern for image, for pause, and purpose-for, in fact, beauty.

Yes, these poems and prose pieces turn on the beauty of poetry, of what art can accomplish. I bid you open the book. It is a miracle.

A Thousand Doors
Matt Pasca
ISBN: 978-0-984568-16-1
Genre: Poetry
116 Pages
Available in paperback and eBook
Price: $13.95 paperback, $4.99 eBook

Poet Matt Pasca explores how personal suffering can be transformed into grace, as if through alchemy, when that grief can be shared with others. Using the Buddhist "Mustard Seed" parable as scaffolding, Pasca's work pays homage to Kisa Gotami's quest to save her son by finding a home where, impossibly, no suffering has befallen the inhabitants. Pasca's poems manuever deftly between the seemingly simple and mundane details of the world around us and the sublime world we often miss in the myopia of our pain.

Dark Salt: A Brush with Genius
Lynn Strongin
ISBN: 978-0-984568-14-7
Genre: Poetry
174 Pages
Available in paperback and eBook
Price: $13.95 paperback, $5.99 eBook

In this collection of late works by Lynn Strongin, we find that perfect balance of salt and water spiced with symbolism and metaphor that poet Strongin does so well. Jewish Temple offerings included salt and Jewish people still dip their bread in salt on the Sabbath as a remembrance of those sacrifices.

In the Language of Women
Charles Adès Fishman
ISBN: 978-0-984568-15-4
Genre: Poetry
152 Pages
Available in paperback and eBook
Price: $13.95 paperback, $4.99 eBook

Charles Adès Fishman focuses entirely on women — their memories, dreams, griefs, triumphs, and visions. *In the Language of Women* honors women's lives and frees the voices of those who have found it difficult, if not impossible, to address actions and events that have wounded and transformed them. It is also a book of fifty-two unforgettable poems in which the distinctive journeys of more than thirty women have been rescued from oblivion and brought to vivid life.

Made in the USA
San Bernardino, CA
11 June 2016